HAIL! ANCIENT GREEKS

Jen Green

Crabtree Publishing Company

www.crabtreebooks.com

Crabtree Publishing Company

www.crabtreebooks.com

Author: Jen Green
Editor: Lynn Peppas
Project coordinator: Kathy Middleton
Production coordinator: Ken Wright
Prepress technician: Ken Wright
Managing editor: Miranda Smith
Designer: Lorna Phillips
Picture researcher: Clare Newman
Design manager: David Poole
Editorial director: Lindsey Lowe
Children's publisher: Anne O'Daly
Consultant: Dr Paul G. Bahn

Photographs:

Alamy: Philip Baran: p. 18 (bottom left); Walter
Bibikow/Danita Delemont: p. 18 (top right);
Tony Wright/Earthscan: p. 25 (center left)
Art Archive: Gianni Dagli Orti, Gianni /
Archaeological Museum Nauplia Nafplion:
p. 27 (bottom center); Alfredo Dagli Orti/
Chiaramaiti Museum, Vatican: p. 28 (center)
Bridgeman Art Library: Sylvia Allouche: p. 12
(center right); Look & Learn: p. 26 (center right);
Look & Learn: p. 27 (center left)

Corbis: Orestis Panagiotou/epa: cover (bottom right);
Ron Watts cover (left); Chris Hellier: p. 25 (center);
Joseph Sohm/Visions of America: p. 10 (center right)
iStockphoto: Syagci: cover (center right); Adrian Beesley:
p. 7 (bottom right); Bill Grove: p. 8 (bottom left);
Image Deport Pro: p. 5 (bottom right), 22/23
(background); Photographer Olympus: p. 25 (top
right); Vonkara1: p. 23 (top right); Marisa Allegra
Willaims: p. 6 (bottom inset)
Mary Evans Picture Library: p. 26 (bottom left)
Photolibrary: Ed Eckstein/Phototake Inc: p. 5 (bottom
center), 19 (bottom right); Roy Rainford/Robert
Harding Picture Library: p. 22 (bottom left)
Thinkstock: p. 21 (center left)
Topham: Luisa Ricciarini: p. 4 (center right);
The Granger Collection: p. 8 (center right),
13 (top right), 19 (center right), 28 (top right),
Art Media/HIP: p. 14 (center right)
Other images by Shutterstock

This book was produced for Crabtree Publishing
Company by Brown Reference Group.

Library and Archives Canada Cataloguing in Publication

Green, Jen
Hail! Ancient Greeks / Jen Green.

(Hail! history)
Includes index.
ISBN 978-0-7787-6623-0 (bound).--ISBN 978-0-7787-6630-8 (pbk.)

1. Greece--Civilization--To 146 B.C.--Juvenile literature.
2. Greece--Social life and customs--Juvenile literature.
I. Title. II. Title: Ancient Greeks. III. Series: Hail! History

DF215.G74 2010   j938   C2010-900825-1

Library of Congress Cataloging-in-Publication Data

Green, Jen.
Hail! Ancient Greeks / Jen Green.
p. cm. -- (Hail! history)
Includes index.
ISBN 978-0-7787-6623-0 (reinforced library binding : alk. paper) --
ISBN 978-0-7787-6630-8 (pbk. : alk. paper)
1. Greece--History--To 146 B.C.--Juvenile literature. 2. Greece--
Civilization--To 146 B.C.--Juvenile literature. I. Title. II. Title: Ancient
Greeks. III. Series.

DF215.G6947 2010
938--dc22
                              2010003031

Crabtree Publishing Company

www.crabtreebooks.com   1-800-387-7650
Copyright © **2011 CRABTREE PUBLISHING COMPANY.**

Printed in China/072010/AP20100226

Published in Canada
Crabtree Publishing
616 Welland Ave.
St. Catharines, Ontario
L2M 5V6

Published in the United States
Crabtree Publishing
PMB 59051
350 Fifth Avenue, 59th Floor
New York, New York 10118

CONTENTS

YOUR GUIDE TO
ANCIENT GREEKS

Welcome to the wonderful world of ancient Greece around 500 BCE. You join us in our Golden Age, when we Greeks lead the world in arts, science, politics, and literature. *HAIL!* reviews our finest achievements so that you, the reader, can judge just what makes Greece great.

LOOKING BACK

History holds the key to our success. *HAIL!* looks back at two great civilizations that paved the way for the Golden Age that we enjoy today.

THIS DAY IN HISTORY: 2,000 BCE

The Minoans dominated Greece from 2200 to 1500 BCE. From their base on the island of Crete, they built a mighty trading empire. Their capital, Knossos, was so upscale that the queen had the world's first flushing toilet!

FLASHBACK: 1000 BCE

The Mycenaeans were a warlike bunch from mainland Greece. They conquered the Minoans and ruled their empire until 1200 BCE. The Mycenaean civilization was made up of small kingdoms—just like the Greece we live in. Their fall was followed by a time of unrest called the Dark Age. Then around 800 BCE, the Golden Age began.

HAIL! QUIZ WHY IS GREECE THE GREATEST?

Enter our readers' poll and select your favorite from these five key achievements.

1. THEATER
Drama began in Greece around 500 BCE. Our plays are performed in open-air theaters. Actors wear masks and platform shoes so that they can be seen from the back row. Our plays will still be put on 2,000 years from now!

2. OLYMPIC GAMES
We Greeks invented athletics as well as the greatest games that the world has ever known. The first Olympics were held in 776 BCE. All competitions are held in the nude! In modern times, they take place every four years.

3. EPIC POETRY
Homer's epic poem the *Iliad*, penned way back around 800 BCE, is one of the finest poems ever written—and certainly one of the longest. It tells of the ten-year war between Greeks and Trojans that began when the Trojan prince Paris stole Helen, wife of King Menelaus of Sparta. The poem ends with the defeat of Troy when the Greeks smuggled troops into the city inside a wooden horse.

4. STRIDES IN SCIENCE
We Greeks are the first people ever to think in the abstract. We practically invented science, philosophy, and history, and made great strides in math and medicine. A little invention called the calculator in 150 BCE will one day pave the way for the computer.

5. DEMOCRACY
Government for the people, by the people, was invented in Athens in 508 BCE. For the first time ordinary people had a say in how the state was run. However, not everyone could vote.

Submit Your Answer

SEE INSIDE:

Gods and Goddesses pp. 8–9

Ask Dr. Hipp p. 19

Olympics pp. 22–23

REGULAR CONTRIBUTORS:
Zeus, Pericles of Athens, Alexander the Great

POSTCARDS FROM....

As readers know well, ancient Greece is not a unified country but a patchwork of city-states, each with its own laws, customs, and unique outlook. Our special roving reporter takes us on a whirlwind tour of the Greek world.

ATHENS

This undisputed capital of culture is also capital of Attica, one of the mightiest of the city-states. A center for arts, learning, and the theater. Awesome temples, of which the Parthenon (see below), perched on the hill of the Acropolis, is cream of the crop.

***HAIL!* says:** *A must for culture-vultures*

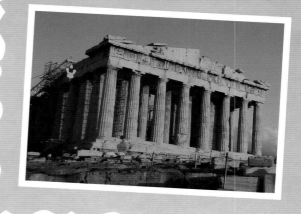

DELPHI

The temple of Apollo on the slopes of Mount Parnassus is one of the holiest spots in Greece. The famous oracle here will reveal your fortune. Known as the navel (belly-button) of Greece.

***HAIL!* says:** *The scenery is pretty cool.*

Did you know?

Corinth was the bustling trading port that had a key location on the narrow neck of land that linked the Peloponnese peninsula with mainland Greece.

SPARTA

The great military state that dominates the southern mainland. Home of tough training and Spartan values (see page 11).

***HAIL!* says:** *Not for softies or simple pleasure seekers*

ITALY

ILLYRIA

THRACE

MACEDONIA

THESSALY

▲ Mount Olympus

■ Troy

ANATOLIA

GREECE

A E G E A N
S E A

ADRIATIC
SEA

Delphi

■ Eretria

ASIA MINOR

SICILY

Thebes ■

■ Athens

Olympia ■

Corinth ■

■ Ephesus

■ Syracuse

PELOPONNESE

■ Mycenae

CYCLADIC
ISLANDS

■ Miletos

Pylos ■

■ Sparta

■ Halikarnassos

M E D I T E R R A N E A N
S E A

■ Knossos

CRETE

The Golden Age in Greece saw the great civilization ruling over lands from Italy in the west to Anatolia in the east.

Did you know?

The temple of Artemis at Ephesus in Asia Minor (now Turkey) was one of the Seven Wonders of the ancient world.

MOUNT OLYMPUS

Home of the Greek gods and the highest mountain in Greece.

HAIL! says: *A must-see for the wildly energetic and the pious at heart*

TROY

Site of the legendary war between the Greeks and Trojans immortalized by Homer. Our victorious soldiers burned the city to the ground, so there's not much to see.

HAIL! says: *Poetry lovers and treasure seekers only. Dusty, windswept plain in Asia Minor*

CRETE

Base of the Minoans, who dominated Greece in early times. Check out the royal palace in the Minoan capital, Knossos.

HAIL! says: *Flattened by a tidal wave, which struck around 1450 BCE, but still impressive. The beaches aren't bad either.*

GREEK GODS &

The ancient Greeks worshiped many gods and goddesses, each of which had different responsibilities. As *HAIL!* readers know, our holy ones have miraculous powers, but are often swayed by all-too-human emotions such as greed, jealousy, anger, lust, and spite.

ARTEMIS

Role: Goddess of hunting and the moon, twin sister of Apollo
Weapon of choice: Bow
Inside story: Artemis has always been a loner. When a human huntsman, Actaeon, peeped in on her bath, she turned him into a stag and his hounds tore him to pieces.

ZEUS

Role: Ruler of gods, Earth, and the heavens—the top job
Weapon of choice: Thunderbolt
Inside story: Zeus has a nasty temper and will hurl a thunderbolt if you cross him. Ladies, beware! He often takes the form of an animal (bull, swan, etc.) to woo mortal girls.

APOLLO

Role: God of the Sun and music
Emblems: Lyre, bow
Inside story: A brilliant musician and expert archer who can see the future. Unfortunately, his latest affair with the mortal Daphne turned very sour.

DAPHNE TELLS ALL

"I wasn't into him. So when he gave chase, I called on the gods, who turned me into a laurel bush."

GODDESSES

ATHENA

Role: Goddess of wisdom, war, and justice

Symbol: An owl

Inside story: The protector of Athens, the warrior goddess Athena has helped many human heroes in her time, including Odysseus, Jason, and Heracles.

TOP GODDESS: Athena gets Hail!'s vote

ARES

Role: God of war, rage, and mindless violence

Symbol: Fire

Inside story: Everyone knows that Ares is in love with Aphrodite, and her husband, Hephaestus the god of blacksmiths, found out. He trapped them in a net for everyone to witness their shame. Serves them right!

POSEIDON

Role: God of the sea, brother of Zeus

Weapon of choice: Trident (three-pronged spear)

Inside story: Poseidon's nose was put out of joint when Zeus got the top job. He can raise storms, earthquakes, and tidal waves, so you need to pray to him before you sail.

HEAD TO HEAD

What's hot and what's not in Athens and Sparta

ATHENS THE BEAUTIFUL

Everyone knows Athens is the world's finest city, famous for its arts, learning, and stunning architecture. Athens is located near the sea, and our navy reigns supreme. Since 478 BCE, Athens has headed a group of states called the Delian League. In fact, the Greeks have taken over now, so it has become the Athenian empire.

TOP INSULT: ATHENS

" **SPARTAN!** "

SHOCK HORROR!
Spartan Babies in Cruelty Scandal

HAIL! has discovered that Spartan babies are tested for strength and fitness. Weak or sickly children are either thrown off a cliff or simply left to die on the mountain. The lucky ones are trained as slaves.

Growing up in Athens

We Athenians pride ourselves on our education. From the age of six, our boys get a thorough training in poetry, music, philosophy, sports, and science—you name it, we teach it! At the age of 18, our well-rounded youths finish off at military college.

In the 400s BCE, two mighty city-states, Athens and Sparta, became deadly rivals. Athens is the home of free speech and culture. Sparta is known for harsh discipline and its tough lifestyle. *HAIL!* profiles the two states in the words of their own people, so you can decide who comes out on top.

SPARTA THE MIGHTY

After a crushing defeat in the 500s BCE, we Spartans vowed never, ever to be defeated again. We have carved out a huge military state run by slaves who are captured in battle. Our strict laws make sure there is no rebellion in the ranks. OK, so our city is a collection of mud huts. And we have no city walls, since we rely on our army for defence. Arts and literature? That's for sissies.

TOP INSULT: SPARTA

" **TREMBLER! COWARD!** "

Growing up in Sparta

Our training is tough. Our boys (and girls) live in barracks from the age of seven and sleep on reeds and thistles. The strongest boys beat the weaker ones to toughen them up. We do not feed them much so they learn cunning by stealing. At 20, our boys are lean, mean fighting machines!

IT'S WAR!

In 431 BCE, Athens and Sparta began a 30-year war to sort out their differences. In 405 BCE, Sparta launched a surprise attack and captured the Athenian navy. Athens was forced to surrender and tear down its walls.

✹

STOP PRESS!

Sparta was so weakened by the long war that it lost to Thebes in 371 BCE.

VOTE FOR ME!

Most Greek city-states were run by a king, nobles, or a top general. Athens was different. In 508 BCE, it set itself up as the world's first democracy—a state ruled by the people. *HAIL!* takes an in-depth look at people-power in Athens. Top politicians reveal why they deserve your vote.

PROCLAMATION
508 BCE

The state of Athens proudly proclaims a

DEMOCRACY

All citizens have the right to vote in the Ekklesia, or Assembly

EXCLUSIONS – *Sorry,* women and slaves are not allowed to vote. No foreigners either. In other words, voting is for wealthy adult males only—*tough luck, everyone else!*

SLAVE BACKLASH!

"They call it the home of democracy, but we slaves make up a third of the population of Athens. For us it is toil, sweat, and tears in the fields, mines, or fine houses from dawn to dusk. We get beaten if we talk back. What a life! It's all right for some, but not for slaves."

Did you know?

Athens is considered to be the birthplace of democracy. The word "democracy" comes from the Greek word that means "power to the people."

VOTE FOR DRACO

★ ★ ★ ★ ★ ★ ★ ★ ★ ★ ★ ★

They say I'm a bit of a stickler. In my day you could be executed for stealing a cabbage or being lazy. I'm only sorry there weren't tougher punishments for real criminals. A vote for me is a vote for law and order.

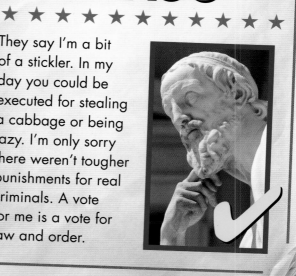

★ WANTED ★

CITIZENS FOR THE ASSEMBLY

Your state needs YOU to pull your weight

- ★ **Duties:** Meet every nine days on Pnyx Hill, but not if it's raining—that's unlucky.
- ★ **Don't be late**—latecomers will be lightly lashed with a rope dipped in red paint.
- ★ **New laws are voted in** with a show of hands.
- ★ **Women, slaves, and foreigners** need not apply.

TOP TIPS FOR ORATORS

- ★ You need a loud voice to make yourself heard. Not too many dramatic gestures.
- ★ If people agree with you they call you an orator. If they disagree, you risk being branded a mob-leader.
- ★ Try to keep your promises—or get really good at covering your tracks.
- ★ Don't get too powerful. You could be banished from Athens if 6,000 people vote against you.

VOTE FOR PERICLES

★ ★ ★ ★ ★ ★ ★ ★

I'm known for my spellbinding speeches. OK, so I was found guilty of stealing public funds, but I did rebuild Athens when it was destroyed by the Persians. I've headed the Assembly every year from 463 to 429 BCE. A vote for me is a vote for Athens!

I VALUE YOUR VOTE!

WANTED FOR JURY SERVICE

- Minimum of 200 citizens needed for each trial—that means you!
- Voting could not be simpler—just drop your bronze token in the guilty or not-guilty box on your way out of the trial.

What's On in GREEKTOWN?

TRAGIC TEAR-JERKER

Top tragedy writer Aeschylus gives us three new plays set during the Trojan War. Greek king Agamemnon sacrifices his daughter to the gods in return for a fair wind to set sail for Troy. On his return, Agamemnon is murdered in his bath by his wife and her lover. In revenge, Orestes, son of Agamemnon, kills his mother…A tale of lust, murder, and revenge.

Homer's Epic Poem

The immortal bard Homer is best known for his epic poem the *Iliad*. It tells of the siege of Troy and the use of the wooden horse, a trick dreamed up by the hero Odysseus. Homer follows this with the *Odyssey*, which details Odysseus' adventures on his journey home. It is a rollicking yarn set on the high seas and exotic islands. Both are destined to become classics!

A SHORT HISTORY OF DRAMA

Athens is the home of theater. The first plays grew from a festival for the god of wine, Dionysus. In the early days, each play had just one voice—a chorus of 12–15 actors all speaking together! We have come a long way since then. Our comedies and tragedies now have up to three actors plus the chorus.

⭐ ⭐ ⭐ ☆ ☆

If arts and the theater are your thing, ancient Greece is the place for you! You can party all year long in Athens, with a steady stream of festivals, athletic competitions, and the play season. *HAIL!* reviews the top shows that are wowing audiences in town.

HAIL! MAGAZINE POLL

Take part in our readers' poll to select your
FAVORITE ENTERTAINMENT

- **TRAGEDY** Plays with unhappy endings, featuring the exploits of gods and heroes. The hero saves the city but dies horribly. **Top writers**: Aeschylus, Euripides, Sophocles. Blood and guts—not for the fainthearted!

- **COMEDY** Plays with happy endings, featuring the everyday lives of ordinary folk. May contain jibes at well-known politicians. **Top writer**: Aristophanes. For all who like their entertainment bawdy, with the rude parts left in.

- **EPIC POEM** Originally orated on stage with a troop of dancers performing. Quality writing. **Top writer**: Homer.

- **FABLE** Stories featuring animals such as hares, tortoises, or foxes. Endings pack a moral punch. **Top writer**: the slave Aesop.

Submit Your Answer

ACTORS WANTED

★ **Men** and **boys** needed for the festival season in Athens and to tour the provinces. **No females**, sorry.

★ You need a **loud voice**, **good memory** for lines, and **stamina** to perform all day.

★ Must be **versatile**—with a maximum of **three actors per play**, you need to take many parts.

★ **Good looks not essential**—you will be wearing a mask and a wig, along with platform shoes to make you taller.

★ Actors rejected for the top parts may apply for the chorus.

Did you know?
The performance area in Greek theaters was a simple, semi-circular space—the orchestra—with the seats rising in tiers on three sides (like this one below).

WELCOME TO MY
BEAUTIFUL HOME!

Wealthy Greek homes have it all—style, comfort, and all the latest gadgets, except for the toilets, which are just a bucket with a seat—if you're lucky! Join *HAIL!*'s style team as we tour some of the best dwellings in ancient Greece.

EXCLUSIVE TOUR

Top athlete Milo of Croton treats *HAIL!* readers to an exclusive peek inside his stylish new home.

My central courtyard is cool and shady in summer, but warm in winter. There is an altar where we offer sacrifices to the gods.

Bedrooms are on the upper floor. Strictly off-limits for journalists, I'm afraid.

The walls may be just mud-brick but they are faced with finest plaster. This color is all the rage this year.

This is the *gynaeceum*, where the women do their thing—spinning, weaving, and gossiping.

This is the *andron*, where we men enjoy lavish banquets. Check out these padded couches! The wife and kids eat here, too, if I don't have guests.

MENU

Sea urchins (right) served with olives, garlic, and radishes
Warning: May contain sharp spikes

- - - - - - - - - -

Poached tuna with herb stuffing, Vine-leaves, fennel, and dandelion (right) salad as side dishes

- - - - - - - - - -

Honey cakes, figs (right), grapes, cheese, and nuts
Warning: May contain traces of nuts

FARMHOUSE, REMOTE PENINSULA, ATTICA

STUNNING!

Detached farmhouse in rural location.
Extensive olive groves.
Easy commuting—only three days journey to Athens.
Plenty of space outside for grazing goats and donkeys.
Great sea view, complete with farmyard smells.

ATHLETE'S WIFE SPEAKS OUT

Milo's wife draws us aside to give her view.

"Being a top athlete's wife is a thankless task, I can tell you. He says my role is to stay home, make clothes, and check on the servants. If I ask too many questions, he orders me to get on with my weaving. I'll give him weaving! He let it slip the other day that things are different in Sparta. The women there have more freedom and are even allowed out in public. I'm tempted to pack my bags."

TOWN HOUSE, CENTRAL ATHENS

MUST SEE!

Deceptively spacious semi just minutes from temples, shops, and marketplace.
Shady central courtyard.
Reception rooms and dining room with a mosaic floor. Kitchen, servants' quarters. No front garden.

YOUR HEALTH

Is your health troubling you? Don't be shy. Our very own doctor, Hippocrates (born around 460 BCE), has all the answers. Doc Hipp is now known as the "father of medicine." Alternatively, you could take the traditional approach and visit the temple of Asklepios, god of medicine.

*Dear Doc Hipp
My tummy is always rumbling.
What can I do?*

Silenus

Dear Silenus
In cases like this I recommend bleeding patients until hardly any blood remains in the body. If you recover from that, you'll be fine.

HIPP'S HINTS FOR TRAINEE DOCTORS

✔ Practice what you preach and keep lean, fit, and healthy. No one likes a flabby doctor.

✔ Dress clean and tidy. A dab of sweet perfume helps to please your patients.

✔ Put on a neutral expression—not too grim and not too jolly.

✔ Act calm and caring—or at least be on your best behavior.

Dear Doc Hipp

My beloved father is worried that he may have a lung disease. Is there any way I can set his mind at rest?

Antigone

Dear Antigone
Give your dad a thorough shaking. If you hear a sloshing sound, then, yes, he probably has a problem with his lungs.

FORGET DOCTORS

Visit the TEMPLE of ASKLEPIOS for your

MIRACLE CURE

Just nod off in the temple. The god will visit you in your dreams and prescribe the cure.
Bring your own pillow. Spa and gym available at our exclusive resort.

Dear Doc Hipp
I suffer from headaches.
Do you have a cure?

Ajax

Dear Ajax
Sure. We drill into the skull and drain off the fluid. We can perform this simple operation at a modest charge. Just drop by anytime.

HIPP'S TOP TIPS FOR A LONG, HEALTHY LIFE

✔ You are what you eat. The Greek diet is pretty healthy really—fish, olive oil, and bread for fiber. Keep eating lots of those fresh fruits and vegetables.

✔ Don't touch the water in cities. Drink weak wine or beer instead.

✔ Take regular exercise to keep fit. It works for me—I'm 89!

HEALTH WARNING 430 BCE GREAT PLAGUE OF ATHENS

Keep away from the city—you have been warned!
Symptoms: Plague starts with sore eyes, a headache, and nausea. Soon you break out in spots, with a burning fever and raging thirst. Most people die, but if you recover, you won't remember a thing about it!

HEAD TO HEAD

We interview the nation's favorite doctor

" The secret of my success? Simple, really. I examine my patients for symptoms, diagnose what's wrong, and prescribe a cure—usually an herbal remedy. It's not all smooth sailing though. Did you know we doctors have to test our patient's urine, mucus, pus, and vomit personally—by tasting it? "

MY FAVORITE IDEAS

No doubt about it, we Greeks are a brainy bunch. Not only have we made huge strides in philosophy, history, politics, and medicine, we also invented see-saws and the yo-yo. *HAIL!* reviews the latest from our great thinkers and sorts the brilliant from the bizarre.

WHO'S WHO?

HAIL! gives a brief guide to Greek philosophers.

1 SOCRATES

When? 469–399 BCE

Most famous pupil: Plato

Best known for: Had writer's block so never wrote anything down. Was found guilty of corrupting Athenians and was forced to commit suicide. Terrible shame.

2 PLATO

When? 429–347 BCE

Most famous pupil: Aristotle

Best known works: *The Republic, Dialogues, Symposium* (the Drinking Party)—see review (right).

3 ARISTOTLE

When? 384–322 BCE

Most famous pupil: Alexander the Great

Best known works: *Physics, Metaphysics, Poetics*

What are they about? Physics, metaphysics, and poetry, of course—what else!

EUREKA
I HAVE IT!

Inventor Archimedes has done it again. Last year, the Egyptian scientist gave us his Archimedes screw to use to draw water from the earth. Now he claims to understand the displacement of water. Says the idea came to him in the bath, of all places. Apparently, he jumped straight out and ran naked down the street shouting "Eureka!" alarming the neighbors. The local court has given him strict instructions to cover up when in public.

CRAZY IDEAS
FROM THE PROVINCES

◆ Xenophanes of Lydia has suggested that fossils are the remains of plants and animals that have turned to stone. Only problem is, a few million years is needed to prove it.

◆ Democritus of Thrace has come up with the idea that all matter is made of tiny particles called atoms. This mad idea will never catch on.

◆ Aristarchus of Samos has suggested that the Earth moves around the Sun, instead of the other way around. Everyone knows the Sun moves around the Earth. Whatever will they think of next?

REVIEW SPOT

Plato's last work, *The Republic*, was a worthy tome about good government. All very fascinating, we're sure, but not high on entertainment value. His new work, the *Symposium* or *Drinking Party*, will be much more to our readers' taste. Mostly about drinking—oh, and ideas of love and beauty. A great read and a must for all those banquets.

OLYMPIC GRANDSTAND

THE GAMES IN OLYMPIA

★ A truce between any warring states is hereby declared in order to guarantee safe conduct for all the athletes and spectators. (*Severe penalties for anyone caught breaking the truce.*)

★ Men and boys only—sorry ladies, but you have your own games in honor of Hera. Any females caught on site will be thrown off the cliff.

★ Athletes from all city-states welcome. Competitors must be naked for all events. No cheating. Anyone caught bribing the judges will be sent home in disgrace.

PROGRAM OF EVENTS

DAY 1
❖ Opening ceremony, sacrifices to Zeus
❖ Oaths by athletes and judges—no crossed fingers or cheating
❖ Trumpeters' competition—very noisy!

DAY 2
❖ Track events including 625 ft (190 m) sprint in full armor
❖ Wrestling, boxing, and pankration—a mixture of both, with only biting and eye-gouging banned

DAY 3
❖ Horse races, chariot races
❖ Pentathlon—five grueling sports: sprint, long jump, javelin, discus, and wrestling

DAY 4
❖ Ceremony in honor of Zeus, with more sacrifices
❖ Athletes' day off to lick wounds

DAY 5
❖ Closing ceremony, winners crowned
❖ Banquet—time to break your diet!
❖ Set off for home

The Olympic Games is Greece's top attraction, held every four years in honor of Zeus. At last, the long wait is over, and the highlight of the sporting calendar is upon us. *HAIL!* brings you all the latest action from Olympia, the home of sports.

WRESTLER KILLED

We report the sad end of Milo of Croton, who won victory in six Olympics, the only athlete ever to do so. On a forest walk, the champ decided to test his strength by ripping a cleft tree in two. Unfortunately his hands got trapped, and several days later, wild animals tore him apart. R.I.P. Milo.

FEMALE IN GAMES SENSATION

A female was unmasked at the Games today. Young Pisidorus had brought along his mother disguised as his trainer. She gave herself away by squealing with delight at her son's victory in the sprint and was led away.

Did you know?

The Olympic flame is lit by the Sun and kept burning until the close of the Games.

DEATH BY DISCUS

Tragedy struck at the Games today when a king was killed by a discus thrown by his own son. The incident has raised questions about safety in the VIP seats at the front.

TRADE & EMPIRE

By 700 BCE, Greek colonies and trading ports were dotted all along the shores of the Mediterranean and Black Seas. Below, *HAIL!* has tracked down the best bargains imported from across the empire, while opposite there are luxury goods available right here in Greece.

Hello, Sailor!

Join the IONIAN FLEET for a life of discovery and adventure. Our ships have been to Spain, Italy, Britain, France, Cyprus, Egypt, Carthage... you name it, we've been there and bought the t-shirt.

YOUR GUIDE TO GREEK TRADE AND EMPIRE

Our trade editor Hermippos gives the lowdown on the top imports and exports around the empire.

PIRAEUS Our chief port. Provides us with our top exports, which are wine, olive oil, silver, and pottery.

THESSALY Known for its wonderful puddings and ribs of beef.

SYRIA Gives us royal purple dye made from whelk shells. The smell from the dye works drifts all over the place!

CARTHAGE The main export is carpets.

LYDIA, ASIA MINOR Famous for its gold mines. The world's first coins were minted here.

HELLESPONT Great for fresh mackerel at the quay.

SHORES OF BLACK SEA Wheat comes from here, the "breadbasket" of the Greek empire.

FRANCE Wine, of course.

SOUTHERN ITALY Main exports are wool and hides. Tanning hides is another smelly industry—hold your nose!

EGYPT Papyrus for paper, sails, cloth, ivory.

ATHENS TEMPLE BUILDERS & QUALITY SCULPTURE

Commission your own temple. Just choose from our three popular styles:

DORIC Simple and sturdy—some say cheap and cheerful.

IONIC Elegant with scroll top—pricier, but you get value.

CORINTHIAN Fancy with leaf decorations. Great if you're rich.

Satisfied customers:
Pericles of Athens, Alexander the Great

We aim to please!

We're rolling prices back!

CLOAKS AND TUNICS

**Latest styles at knockdown prices
Fine or coarse linen
Wide range of colors:**

pink, blue, saffron yellow, or regal purple

One size fits all

NEW THEATER OPENS 272 BCE

The brand new theater at Dodona opened this week to packed audiences. The amphitheater is horseshoe-shaped and seats up to 14,000 spectators. Book the royal seats at the bottom for a great view of the stage. The top tiers are for those with good eyesight.

HURRY
WHILE STOCKS LAST

Pheidias the butcher proudly announces a GRAND SALE of sacrificial animals on the eve of the festival of Zeus. Wide choice of animals for slaughter, such as pigs, goats, sheep, cows, or aurochs.

To suit any pocket

INTO BATTLE

The Greeks produced thinkers such as scientists and doctors, but they also had great warriors who built an empire. The Trojan War was the Greeks' most famous epic battle, but they fought many a good fight after that. *HAIL!* presents a pull-out guide to great battles with their arch-enemies, the Persians.

GREAT GREEK BATTLES

by General Themistocles of Athens

MARATHON
1

When? 490 BCE
Who? Persians vs Athens
What happened? Our troops were outnumbered ten to one on the plain of Marathon. Our runner, Pheidippides, ran 155 miles (250 km) to ask the Spartans for help but they dragged their feet—something about a festival. Anyway, two flanks of our finest managed to surround the Persians, who panicked. The result: 6,400 Persians dead, with the loss of only 192 Athenians. Pheidippides ran 25 miles (40 km) to Athens (left) to announce our victory, then unfortunately dropped dead.

THERMOPYLAE
2

When? 480 BCE
Who? Persians vs Spartans
What happened? A Spartan force of just 300 men led by King Leonidas defended the narrow pass of Thermopylae against the might of the Persian army. They were eventually massacred but put on a terrific show, which inspired the rest of us for years! You have to hand it to the Spartans, they are good in a scrap.

SPARTA EXPECTS

HAIL!'s reporter got the exclusive on Spartan General Leonidas' pep talk to his heroic men on the eve of Thermopylae:

" Now men, we're in a tight corner. They may massively outnumber us, but remember, we are Spartans, and they're only Persians. They say they will send a hail of arrows to blot out the Sun. No worries—we like a bit of shade when we're fighting! Don't forget to oil your body and comb your hair before the battle. We may all be massacred, but at least we'll die looking good! "

SEA BATTLE OF SALAMIS

3

When? 480 BCE

Who? Persians vs Greeks

What happened? In this famous sea battle, the Persian fleet outnumbered our ships by three to one. But we managed to lure the Persians into a narrow strait. Then our heavy warships, called triremes, rammed the flimsy Persian vessels and sank all of them. Good riddance, I say! That finished off the Persian threat for years.

ALEXANDER THE GREAT

MODEL PUPIL

by ARISTOTLE, PHILOSOPHER

Young Alexander was my star pupil. His dad took me on as his tutor in 343 BCE. Alex loved Homer's poetry. He carried a copy of the *Iliad* with him wherever he went on all his campaigns.

MY DAD by Alex

My father, Philip of Macedon, was a brilliant general. When he inherited Macedon it was a backwater. By 338 BCE, he had conquered the rest of Greece and made it one country. He was killed by his own bodyguard. People say I was behind it, but that's a lie!

MY BRILLIANT CAREER

General Alex talks you through the key events in his 11-year campaign to conquer the known world.

MACEDON (Macedonia) Home, sweet home
TYRE A tough nut to crack, but we took it after a siege in 332 BCE
BATTLE OF ISSUS One of my most brilliant victories against the Persians in 333 BCE
EGYPT Conquered in 332 BCE—easy!
BATTLE OF GAUGAMELA I polished off the Persians here in 331 BCE.
326 BCE Defeated a huge Indian army including 200 elephants
324 BCE Forced to turn back after mutiny by my own men—the swines!
PERSEPOLIS I burned this Persian city to the ground after a drinking binge—oops!

Roxanne, Persian Princess

I married Alex in 327 BCE, after he conquered my people. I was just 16. He said it was to cement friendship between Greece and Persia. Now he's pretending to be Persian! He's even kept on the Persian king's harem of 365 women.

Of all the great Greeks, Alexander (356—323 BCE) is the greatest. Hailing from remote Macedonia in northern Greece, he succeeded his father, Philip of Macedon, to the throne in 336 BCE. By the age of only 32, he had conquered the largest empire the world has ever known, stretching from Greece to India, and south to Egypt.

MUTINY IN THE RANKS

A common soldier reveals all

Alex is our hero. We were happy to follow him as far as India, but he wanted to press on even further. We decided enough was enough and went on strike. He sulked in his tent for three days, but then he had to turn back. Mutiny was the only way to make him see sense.

ME, BIG-HEADED?

"People say I've got big-headed. True, I've named 16 cities Alexandria after me, and one after my horse Bucephalus. Yes, I know I'm the first ruler to put my head on a coin. And yes, I did kill a friend who refused to worship me as a god. But I was a bit tipsy and besides, I've got to keep up standards among my followers."

END OF AN ERA

HAIL! reports the sad end of Alexander, who died of a fever in Babylon in 323 BCE. Critics say that he'd had one binge too many. His empire is to be divided between three of his generals. Ptolemy gets Egypt, Antigonus has Greece, and Seleuceus takes Asia.

STOP PRESS: GREECE CONQUERED BY ROME!

"We Romans are top dogs now. We conquered Alexander's empire between 164 and 146 BCE. Our army's the best, but don't get us wrong—we love Greek culture. We've copied Greek arts, architecture, science, and even their gods. They say we're more Greek than the Greeks!"

GLOSSARY

Acropolis The hilltop fortress of Athens, where there is a temple called the Parthenon

andron A dining room in a private home, usually used by men only

auroch A type of huge wild cattle in Europe, Asia, and North America; now extinct

backwater A place considered isolated or backward; not forward-moving

bawdy Something indecent or obscene

citizen A free man who belonged to a city-state

city state A city that ruled the land around it

Dark Age A period of war and unrest in Greece that lasted from about 1200 to 800 BCE

Delian League An alliance of city-states, headed by Athens, that was founded in 478 BCE

democracy Rule by the people; the city of Athens established the world's first democracy

Ekklesia The assembly in Athens that voted in new laws

eureka "I have it" in ancient Greek

Golden Age Classical period of ancient Greece when arts, science, and learning flourished

gynaeceum Women's rooms in a private house in Greece

hoplite A Greek foot soldier armed with a long spear, round shield, and short sword

Ionia An ancient region of Anatolia in modern-day Turkey

Minoans The civilization from Crete that dominated Greece from 2200 to 1500 BCE

Mycenaeans The warlike race who ruled ancient Greece from 1500 to 1200 BCE

oracle A holy place where the Greeks believed the gods spoke to humans and told their future

orator A public speaker, especially one who speaks with great eloquence

pankration A Greek sport, a mixture of boxing and wrestling—very rough!

pentathlon An athletic event made up of five sports

Persia A mighty empire that fought wars with ancient Greece from 500 to 449 BCE

philosophy A Greek word meaning love of wisdom

trireme A Greek warship mainly powered by three banks of oars

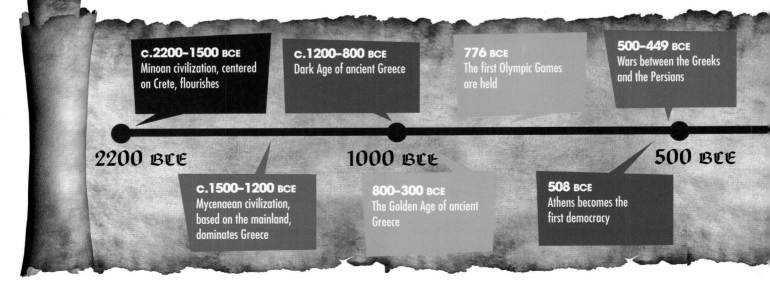

c.2200–1500 BCE
Minoan civilization, centered on Crete, flourishes

c.1200–800 BCE
Dark Age of ancient Greece

776 BCE
The first Olympic Games are held

500–449 BCE
Wars between the Greeks and the Persians

2200 BCE   1000 BCE   500 BCE

c.1500–1200 BCE
Mycenaean civilization, based on the mainland, dominates Greece

800–300 BCE
The Golden Age of ancient Greece

508 BCE
Athens becomes the first democracy

ON THE INTERNET

The comprehensive Kidipede site that looks at all aspects of life in ancient Greece, including government, architecture, religion, sports and games, clothing, and mythology
www.historyforkids.org/learn/greeks/

A primary history source of information on ancient Greece for students and teachers. Includes activities, photographs, fun facts, and links to other sites
www.bbc.co.uk/schools/ primaryhistory/ancient_greeks/

The British Museum, London, Web site about ancient Greece, including stories and questions to extend knowledge
www.ancientgreece.co.uk/

Detailed history of Alexander's life, reign, and military campaigns with maps and photographs
www.livius.org/aj-al/alexander/ alexander00.html

Greek gods and goddesses and related topics. Includes quizzes and puzzles
www.greek-gods.info/greek-gods/

A timeline of events in ancient Greece
http://ancient-greece.org/resources/ timeline.html

BOOKS

Life in Ancient Greece (Peoples of the Ancient World) by Lynn Peppas (Crabtree Publishing, 2004)

If I Were a Kid in Ancient Greece (Children of the Ancient World) by Cobblestone Publishing (Cricket Books, 2007)

Ancient Greece by Anne Pearson (Dorling Kindersley, 2007)

Tools of the Ancient Greeks: A Kid's Guide to the History & Science of Life in Ancient Greece by Kris Bordessa (Nomad Press, 2006)

Cleopatra by Adele Geras (Kingfisher, 2007)

Adventures in Ancient Greece by Linda Bailey (Kids Can Press, 2002)

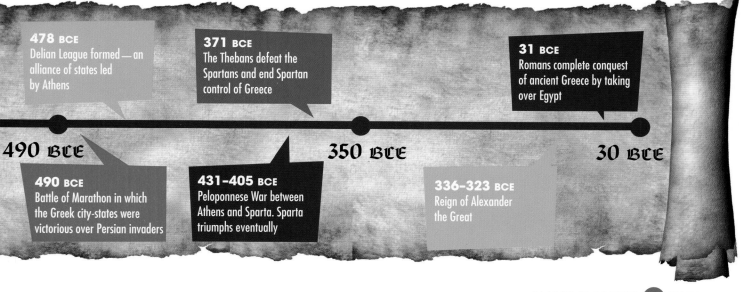

478 BCE
Delian League formed—an alliance of states led by Athens

371 BCE
The Thebans defeat the Spartans and end Spartan control of Greece

31 BCE
Romans complete conquest of ancient Greece by taking over Egypt

490 BCE   350 BCE   30 BCE

490 BCE
Battle of Marathon in which the Greek city-states were victorious over Persian invaders

431–405 BCE
Peloponnese War between Athens and Sparta. Sparta triumphs eventually

336–323 BCE
Reign of Alexander the Great

INDEX